FLUTE

Compiled and Edited by Mizzy Mc(

MW00824652

MEL BAY PRESENTS
FLUTE DUETS

Volume I: Works by Devienne, Hotteterre, Loeillet, Meline, Stamitz, & Telemann

1 2 3 4 5 6 7 8 9 0

CONTENTS

Twenty Four Progressive Duets (1821)

Florant Meline

Allegro

Allegretto

Rondo
Allegretto

Menuetto con Var.

Var. 1

Var. 2

Var. 3

16

Sonata I

Jean–Baptiste Loeillet
(1680 –1730)

Fine

D.C. al Fine

Sonata IV

Jean-Baptiste Loeillet
(1680 –1730)

Gavotte

Sarabanda Largo

Sonata VI

Jean-Baptiste Loeillet
(1680-1730)

Duo I

Francois Devienne
(1759-1803)

Rondeau

Allegro

Duo II

Francois Devienne
(1759-1803)

Menuetto

Duo III

Francois Devienne
（1759-1803）

Presto

Fine

D.C. al Fine

41

Duo IV

Devienne

Grazioso

Duo V

Devienne

47

NOTES ON PERFORMANCE

The following duet by Hotteterre belongs to an era marked by highly stylized performance practices. More often than not the contemporary flutist is unfamiliar with rules of performance that 18th century Baroque masters observed. While many types of ornamentation were notated in the music not all of the ornaments necessary for a tasteful performance were indicated. The refined skill of ornamenting in the Baroque style requires knowledge, experience, and musical sensitivity, all of which come through practice and thoughtful study.

For additional information on Baroque performance practices see:

Donington, Robert. The Interpretation of Early Music. London: Faber and Faber, 1974.
Hotteterre, Jacques. Principles of the Flute, Recorder, and Oboe. Translated and edited by David Lasocki. London: Barrie and Rockliff, 1968. (or. pub. 1707).
Lasocki, David and Betty Bang Mather. Interpretation of French Music from 1675 to 1775. New York: McGinnis and Marx, 1973.
Quantz, Johann Joachim. On Playing the Flute. Translated and edited by Edward R. Reilly. New York: The Free Press, 1966.
Veilhan, Jean-Claude. The Rules of Musical Interpretation in the Baroque Era. Paris: Alphonse Leduc, 1979.

RHYTHMIC ALTERATION

Performance practices of 18th century French musicians included the use of notes inégales or unequal notes. This was a type of rhythmic inequality which permitted the uneven performance of evenly notated values.

For example: in a pair of notes the first is stressed and the second is shortened

The degree of inequality was left up to the performer.

INEQUALITY IN VARYING METERS

Movement from Hotteterre Suite	Time Signature	Notes played unequally when moving by steps or small leaps
Gravement	¢	Sixteenth (Semi-Quaver)
Allemande	C	Sixteenth (Semi-Quaver)
Rondeau	2	Eighth (Quaver)
Gigue	6/8	Sixteenth (Semi-Quaver)
Passacaille	3/4	Eighth (Quaver)

To cancel notes inégales, or to ensure the equal performance of note values, composers would give directions as follows:

1) Les croches égales - meaning ♪ notes played equally, ♪ notes played unequally (see Hotteterre Suite - 1st movement)

2) dots or strokes over the noteheads ꜛ ꜛ (not to be confused with staccato) (see Hotteterre Suite - 3rd movement)

ARTICULATION

Varying articulation patterns aid in the unequal grouping of notes. The preferred articulation pattern used by Hotteterre was called a tongue stroke or tongue slur, and alternated the syllables tu and ru. To approximate these syllables use doo and du, where doo is a strong pulse and du a weaker one.

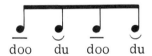

doo   du   doo   du

Hotteterre summarizes the appropriate use of ornaments in his Pièces pour la flûte traversière et autres instruments, avec la basse continue. Livre Premier. Oeuvre Second. 1708.

You should observe that it is necessary to make flattements on almost all long notes, and to do them (as well as tremblements and battements) slower or quicker according to the tempo and character of the piece.

That you must make a coulement in all descending intervals of thirds.

That you often do a double cadence when you ascend one note higher after a tremblement.

You can scarcely determine all the places where the accent must be placed. You do it normally at the end of a dotted crochet when it is followed by a quaver at the same pitch (in time signatures where the quavers are equal). You do them on certain long notes, but you must use them rarely.

ORNAMENTS

Coulé	$\frown$	Passing appogiatura. Played before rather than on the beat. Used on descending intervals of a third.
Port de voix simple	$\smile$	Single appogiatura. Ascends by step to the following note.
Port de voix double	/	Double appogiatura. Ascends by step to the following note. Sometimes called a slide.
Battement	I	Pincé or mordent. A rapid alternation of the principal note and the note below.
Tremblement	+	Cadence, trill, or shake. Rapid alternation of the principal note and the note above. Usually begins on the note above.
Tremblement simple	+	Trill without preparation.
Tremblement appuyé	$\hat{+}$	Called a "prepared" trill. Upper note is prolonged to delay the trill.
Tremblement tourne	$\underset{+}{\infty}$	Double cadence. Trill with two closing notes, one a whole or half step below the principal note, and the other the principal note.
Cadential trill	+	Always added to the dominant chord at a full cadence. A prepared trill that is closed with two notes.
Tour de gosier	∞	Doublé, turn, or grupetto. A turn around the main note; i.e. the note above, the main note, the note below, and a return to the main note.
Plainte	/	Accent. Added at the end of a note. Above the principal note.
Tour de chant	$\cup$	A melodic turn used as preparation for a trill.
Flattement (usually not indicated)	$\wedge\wedge$	Vibrato. Produced by shaking the fingers over the vented tone holes. Performed on all long notes ($\circ$, ρ , $\rho\cdot$) The modern flute limits this technique.
Chûte	\	Joins an upper note to a lower note by dropping with an anticipation of the lower one.

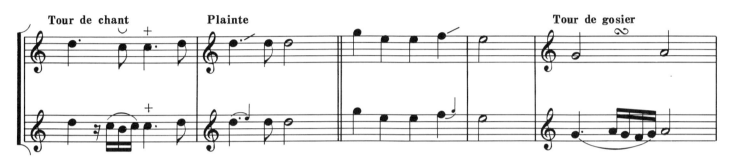

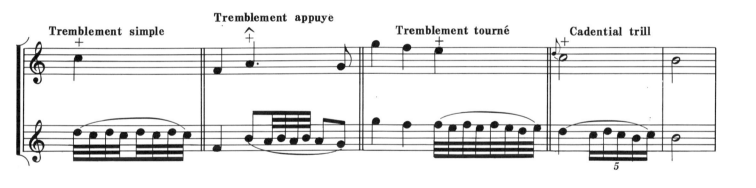

Duo from Première suitte de pièces a deux dessus
Suite I, Op. 4 (1712)

Jacques Hotteterre
(1680 – 1761)

Gay Les Croches égales

55

ALLEMANDE.

Gay

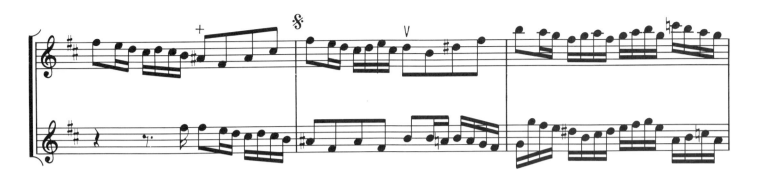

RONDEAU, Tendre. Les Tourterelles.

Gracieusement, et un peu lent.

RONDEAU, Gay.

61

GIGUE.

PASSACAILLE.

from Six Duo Concertans pour Deux Flutes
Duo I

Anton Stamitz
(1754–1809)

74

D.C. al Fine

Excerpts from Six Sonatas or Duets for Two German Flutes or Violins, Op. 2

Sonata II

Georg Philipp Telemann
(1681–1761)

Sonata III

Georg Philipp Telemann
(1681-1761)

Affetuoso